JOURNEY INTO CIVILIZATION
ANCIENT CHINA

by Robert Nicholson and Claire Watts

CHELSEA JUNIORS
A division of Chelsea House Publishers
New York • Philadelphia

Editorial consultant: Dr Anne Farrer,
Department of Oriental Antiquities, British Museum

This edition published 1994 by Chelsea House Publishers, a division of Main Line Book Co.
300 Park Avenue South, New York, N.Y. 10010 by arrangement with Two-Can Publishing Ltd.
This edition copyright © Two-Can Publishing Ltd., 1994

First published in Great Britain in 1991 by Two-Can Publishing Ltd., 346 Old Street, London EC1V 9NQ
Original edition © Two-Can Publishing Ltd 1993

1 3 5 7 9 8 6 4 2

ISBN 0-7910-2702-3
ISBN 0-7910-2726-0 (pbk.)

Photographic credits:
Werner Forman: p1, p8, p9, p11, p20, p24, p30(c); Sonia Halliday: p5, p13; Toby Maudsley; p17, p23; Ronald Sheridan; p11, p12, p15, p18, p19(1), p21;
John Stevens: p30(t), p30(b); ET Archive: p19; Zefa; p6, p7
Illustration credits:
Jon Davis/Linden Artist: p4; Malcolm Stokes/Linden Artists: p6, p8, p9, p10, p12, p14, p15, p16, p17, p18, p20, p21, p22,p 24; Maxine Hamil: Cover, pp25-29

Contents

All words that appear in **bold** can be found in the glossary.

silk route

Anyang. The earliest Chinese city that has been discovered. Dates back to 1300 B.C.

Great Wall

Beijing

area of loess soil

Yellow River

Xian Yang

The capital city of the first Qin emperor, Qin Shi Huang Di.

Yangzi River

The Ancient Chinese World

China was a united country with big cities and a system of government before the great European **civilizations**, the Greeks and the Romans, had even begun to spread across Europe. By about 1766 B.C. one family had grown so powerful that it managed to take over the lands of local lords. This family ruled China for 700 years. Other families have ruled China since then. The period of time when a family ruled is known as a **dynasty**. One of the most famous is the Qin dynasty, which China is named after.

Chinese Lands

China is a huge country, stretching over 1800 miles from the mountains and ice of Tibet in the west through forests and deserts to the tropical coastline of the east.

Chinese civilization first began around the Yellow River in the center of the country, where the soil is a rich yellow earth called **loess**. This fertile earth has been blown onto the land by the wind over thousands of years.

The ancient Chinese discovered that they could grow good crops on this loess only if it was kept well watered. They developed a system of **terraces** cut into the hillsides to make the most of the land. In the north, wheat was the main crop, and in the south, where there was more water, rice was grown in flooded fields called paddies.

Peasant farmers provided food for the entire Chinese empire but usually had scarcely enough to eat themselves. Crops often failed, causing periods of great famine. Sometimes the starving peasants rebelled against the rich landlords.

⬕ Complex irrigation systems were set up to water the fields.

▶ Terraces were cut into the hillsides to make the most of every bit of land.

The Great Wall

The Great Wall of China was built to protect China's northern border from invading tribes. In 221B.C. the new emperor, Qin Shi Huang Di, sent 30,000 men to start building the wall. From then on emperor after emperor extended and rebuilt it right up to this century. The wall was made of pounded earth covered with stones. It was wide at the bottom and narrowed at the top, where there was a walkway for guards. The length of the wall was broken at intervals by watchtowers.

▲ Traders used to travel along China's northern border, taking their **silk** to India, the Middle East and Europe.

▲ According to a Chinese legend, the Great Wall is really a huge dragon turned to stone.

Great Wall Facts

● The wall is between 16 feet and 32 feet high.
● The walkway along the top is 16 feet wide.
● Watchtowers are located every 290 feet to 585 feet along the wall.
● The wall originally stretched for 3,700 miles along China's border.

▶ Cross section of the Great Wall.

The Forbidden City

China was one of the first countries in the world to have large numbers of people living close to one another in cities. Chinese cities were built with walls all around them to protect them from enemies. Inside the most important city, the emperor had a palace which also had high walls, creating a city within a city.

For example, during the Ming dynasty, the emperor Yongle rebuilt China's main city,

Beijing. By this time Beijing had a million inhabitants. Inside the city walls was a walled imperial city where the important government officials lived and worked. Inside this area was a palace known as the Forbidden City – also surrounded by a high wall – where the emperor lived. At night no man other than the emperor was allowed inside the walls.

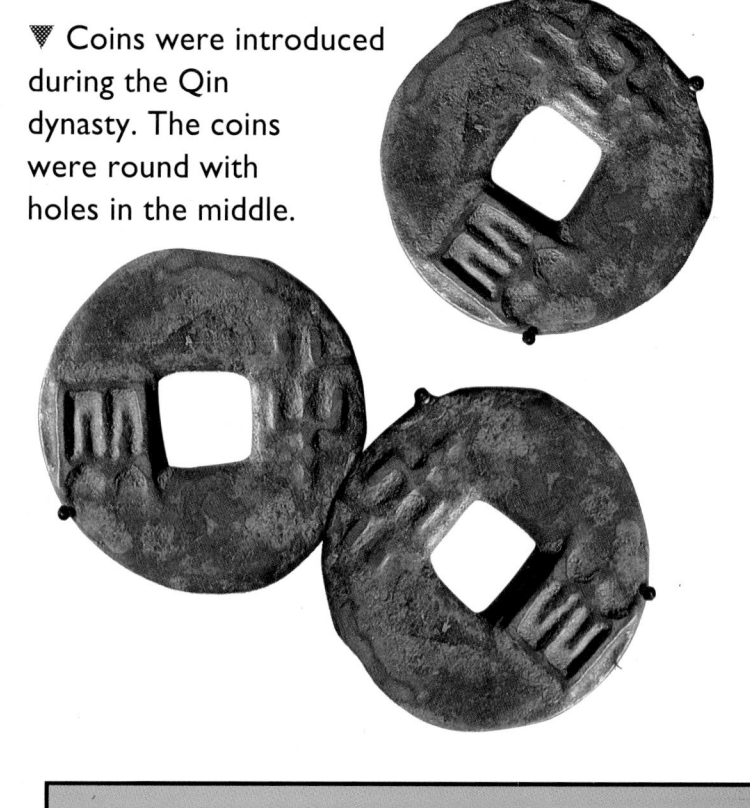

▼ Coins were introduced during the Qin dynasty. The coins were round with holes in the middle.

Government

The first Chinese emperors gave huge estates all over China to their friends and relatives and enlisted their support to help govern the country. However, these lords often became too powerful for the emperor to control and civil war would break out. In the Qin dynasty, the emperors set up a form of **civil service** to govern the country instead. People who wanted to join the civil service had to take very difficult exams to prove that they could do the job.

▼ People walking along the long, straight road to the Forbidden City could be seen long before they arrived at the gates.

City Life

The Chinese believed that the world was square, so they built their cities to reflect this, laid out in regular patterns, with straight streets crossing each other at right angles. This divided the town into squares, known as *wards*. Usually the houses of the rich would be found at one end, near the palace, and those of the poor at the other end.

The poor people had houses built from mud and thatch. To keep out drafts in winter, the houses were built with floors below ground level, and blankets were hung over the windows and doors. In the center of the house was a sunken pit containing the fire, but there was no chimney to let out the smoke.

Rich people's houses were built around huge courtyards. They were made of painted wood, and roofed with pottery tiles. They contained little furniture – straw mattresses which were rolled up during the day, cushions rather than chairs, and big chests and cupboards.

▼ Chinese houses had curved roofs designed to keep away evil spirits. Spirits were believed to travel in straight lines and it was thought that the curved roofs would confuse them!

Festivals

Most Chinese people worked very hard and had no weekends or other days off. Instead there were festivals throughout the year, which were celebrated with processions and dancing in the street. Fireworks would be let off, kites flown, and people would dress up in dragon costumes, because dragons were supposed to represent fun and excitement.

▶ Dragons and other grotesque creatures were supposed to protect the house and bring good luck.

Inventions

Chinese scientists discovered many things that have made great changes to civilization throughout the world. They were interested in medicine, navigation, chemistry and, of course, they were always trying to improve agriculture to feed the enormous population.

Fireworks and Rockets

Chinese inventors discovered the formula to make **gunpowder**. This was first used to make firebombs. It is likely that the Chinese also made the earliest cannons.

The Wheelbarrow

The Chinese invented all sorts of lifting apparatus, including the wheelbarrow, which they called a wooden ox.

Compass

The Chinese discovered magnetism and made **compasses** by floating magnets in bowls of water. They were used for navigation, and to check that a new building faced in a direction that would bring good fortune.

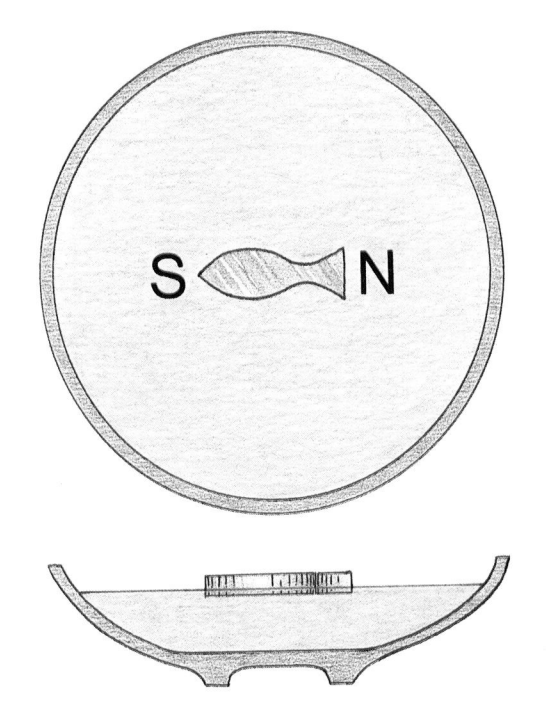

▲ This huge waterwheel powered the giant water clock.

Clocks

Clocks were another Chinese invention. Giant water clocks were invented that rang every 15 minutes to record the passing of the day for the royal officials. The records of this invention were kept so carefully that modern clock makers have been able to use them to reconstruct the clocks.

Medicine

Chinese doctors were very good at treating various illnesses. They invented some cures which are still used today, such as kaolin, made from powdered clay, for an upset stomach. They often treated illness with **acupuncture**. Needles were placed into the skin in particular places on the body to cure problems in other parts of the body. Many people still use acupuncture today to help with certain illnesses.

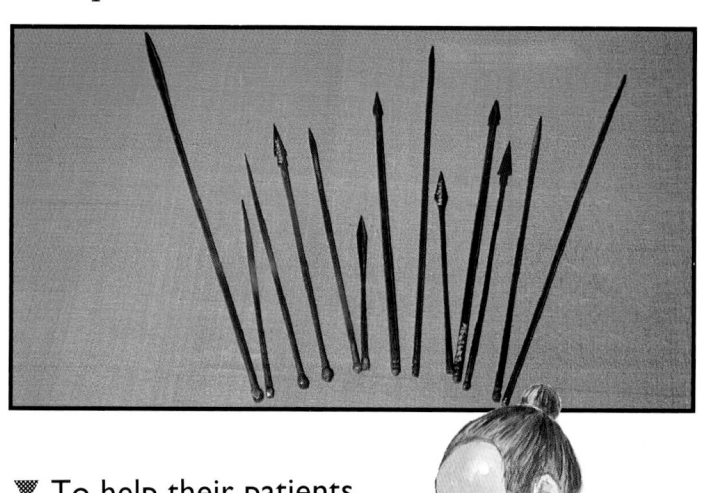

▼ To help their patients, doctors had to know exactly where in the body to place one of these needles.

Paper

Perhaps the greatest Chinese invention of all was paper and, with it, printing.

The earliest Chinese writing has been found carved on animal bones. After this, the Chinese began to paint on bamboo strips and silk. In about A.D.100 paper was invented. Wood pulp, hemp and other waste materials were mashed up, mixed with water, rolled, stretched and dried in the sun to form paper. Paper was the cheapest writing material, and it was much quicker and easier to write on than anything people had used before.

Within a few hundred years the Chinese had developed a form of printing. Wooden blocks carved with lines of text were rubbed with ink and then paper was smoothed over them. This was much quicker than writing books by hand and copies could be made very easily.

Chinese Writing

Chinese letters are different from ours. Each of our letters represents a sound, and for them to mean anything we have to combine them to make up a word. Chinese letters are called characters. They do not represent sounds but meanings. At first some characters were pictures that could very easily be understood, but gradually the signs became simpler, to make them quicker and easier to write.

EARLY CHARACTERS	MODERN	ENGLISH
山	山	mountain
⊖	日	sun
⟩	月	moon
馬	馬	horse

Cutting reeds and soaking them

Mashing the pulp

Make Your Own Printing Block

The ancient Chinese carved their printing blocks out of wood, but here's an easier way to do it! Draw a design and trace it. Cut several copies of the design out of lightweight cardboard and glue them, one on top of another, to a piece of heavy cardboard, so that the design is raised above the surface. Cover your printing block with ink or paint and press onto a sheet of paper.

Always ask a grown-up to help you when you use sharp scissors.

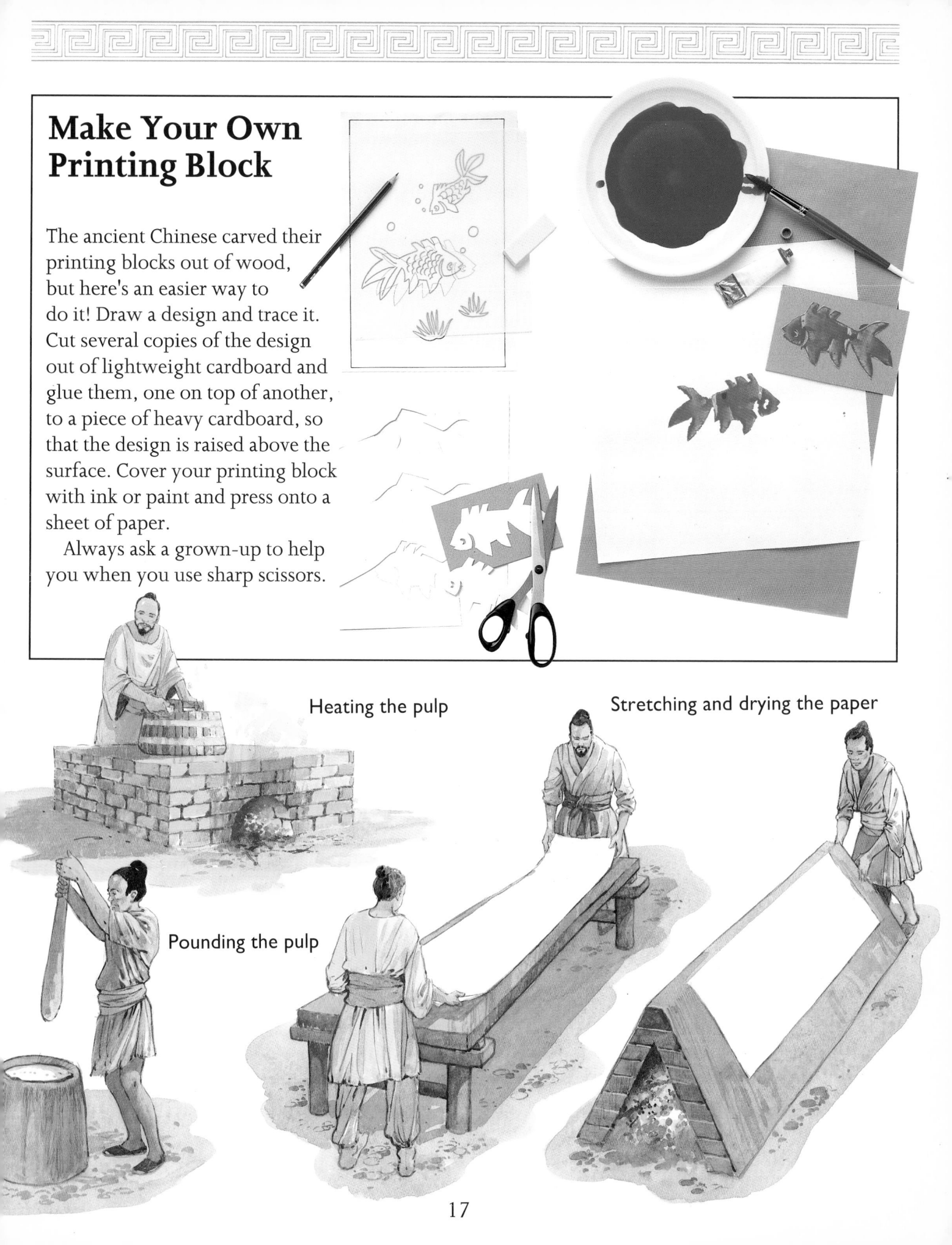

Heating the pulp

Stretching and drying the paper

Pounding the pulp

Great Thinkers

The Chinese did not believe in a single all-powerful god, and the government never tried to force the people to practice one religion. People believed that different religions could exist together in harmony. Most Chinese thought that the balance of nature was delicate and that everything had an opposite side that was very important. They called the two opposite forces that governed everything **yin** and **yang**. A balance of these was thought to bring peace, joy, and order.

Buddhism

Buddha taught people that they should free themselves of all worldly desires in order to gain perfect happiness, or *nirvana*. **Buddhism**, which originally came from India, became China's most popular religion.

18

Taoism

Confucius thought that people were the most important element in the world, but another great thinker, **Lao-tsu** developed **Taoism**. This taught that people were only one element among thousands that make up the world and that they should try to fit in with the ways of the universe rather than change them.

Kung-Fu-tsu

The most famous Chinese **philosopher, Kung-Fu-tsu** (often known as Confucius), lived during the Chou dynasty. He taught that people could only live together happily and peacefully if they followed the rules that he set down in a book called the **Analects**. He believed that it was very important to respect other people, and one of his teachings was *do to other people as you would like them to do to you*. The teachings of Confucius developed into the empire's main religion.

Crafts

The Chinese were experts in many crafts. They produced beautiful objects in metal, stone, and pottery.

Jade

Jade is a hard, green stone that was considered very valuable by the Chinese. They believed it represented five essential virtues: charity, trustworthiness, courage, wisdom, and fairness. This funeral suit is made from 2,000 pieces of jade threaded together with gold-covered wire.

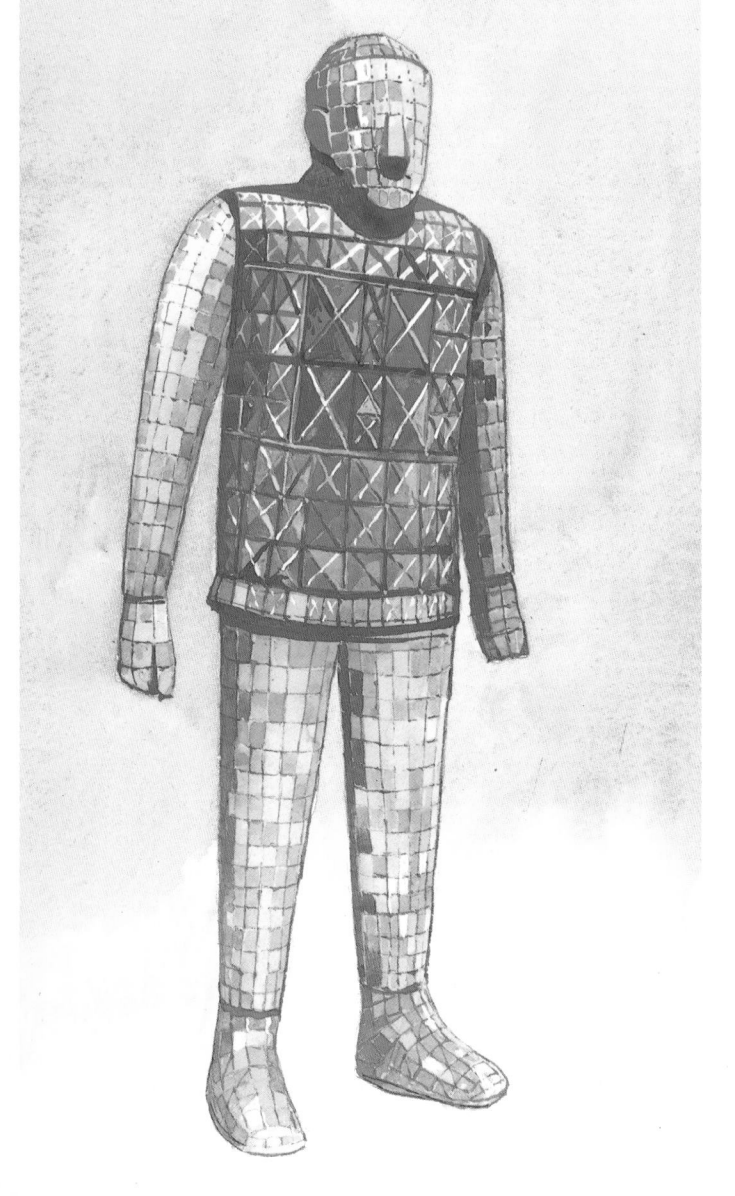

China

The Chinese invented **porcelain,** a fine-grained type of ceramic, which we still call *china.* They decorated it with delicate patterns and colors.

Gardens

Gardening was regarded as a great art. Chinese cities were designed to include peaceful gardens and parks. Each item in the garden was thought to have a different meaning: water lilies represented truth; chrysanthemums, culture; and bamboo, strength.

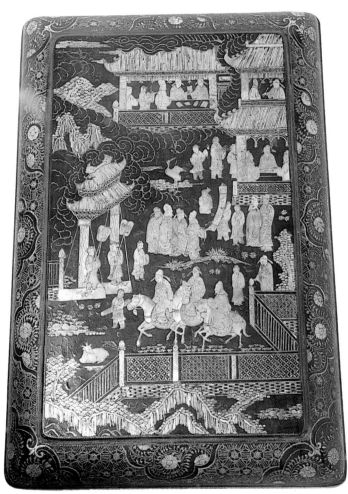

Silk

The Chinese kept the secret of silk making to themselves for many years. Silk thread comes from the cocoon of a type of caterpillar, which has to be carefully cared for and fed on mulberry leaves. The cloth made from this thread was the source of China's trade with other countries.

Lacquer

Lacquer is made from the sap of a special type of oak tree. When heated, the sap becomes hard and shiny like glass. It was used with dyes to decorate houses and furniture.

Food

Rich Chinese people had an exciting and varied diet. They ate a wide variety of meat, like ox, mutton, deer, pig and even dog. The most common dish was a rich stew called *geng*. Meals contained lots of small courses and sometimes a big feast would go on for half a day. There might be 300 different dishes to choose from at a feast, including delicacies like bears' paws, baked owl and bird's nest soup.

Poor people often struggled to eat enough to stay alive. Their geng usually contained only vegetables. People in the north ate a lot of a cereal called millet, and in the south they ate rice. They also ate bean curd, noodles and bread.

Food was eaten out of small bowls using chopsticks and weak green tea was drunk with it. The rich drank wine made from rice.

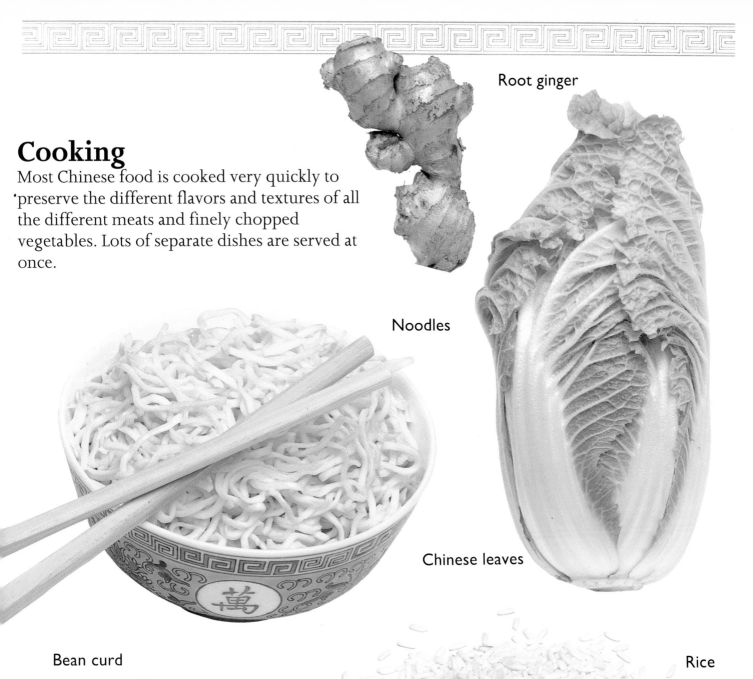

Cooking

Most Chinese food is cooked very quickly to preserve the different flavors and textures of all the different meats and finely chopped vegetables. Lots of separate dishes are served at once.

Root ginger

Noodles

Chinese leaves

Bean curd

Rice

▲ Although poor Chinese people ate mostly bland rice and bean curd, they added strong-flavored spices and ginger to them to make them taste better.

Clothes

Rich and poor people in China wore very different clothes. Poor men wore baggy **hemp** trousers with a loose shirt over the top and a fur-lined coat in winter. The women wore simple dresses made from wool in winter and cotton in summer. Their shoes were made from woven straw.

Rich men and women wore robes of silk tied at the waist with a large sash. The front of a woman's robe was opened a little to reveal an undershirt of different-colored silk. They wore silk slippers with wooden soles on their feet.

▼ This embroidered badge would have been worn by an official to show his rank.

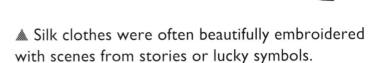

▲ Silk clothes were often beautifully embroidered with scenes from stories or lucky symbols.

Mothers carried small babies on their backs in a fold of their dresses until the babies were old enough to walk. From then on they wore miniature versions of adult clothes.

Both men and women had long hair. Most people wore this in a topknot, but rich women had their hair dressed in elaborate shapes and decorated with jeweled combs. People only cut their hair when a close family member died.

The Dragon King's Key

The ancient Chinese told many stories about the world around them.
Although these stories are not true we can find out about life in ancient China from them.
The Dragon King's Key is a tale about a drought.

The rains around Horse Ear Mountain were very scarce one year. The land was so dry that the crops would not grow and the people who lived at the foot of the mountain had nothing to eat. The river dried up and people began to think that they would have to leave their homes or die.

One day, when she was walking on the mountain, a farmer's daughter called Sea Girl came upon a secret lake. She could see the lake shining between the mountain peaks and smell the cool breeze that rippled its surface, but she could not reach the water.

As she stared longingly at the lake, a wild goose flew down beside her.

"I am the Guardian of the Lake," said the wild goose. "It is impossible to reach the shining

waters. They are locked in with a golden key that is hidden in a fortress far away."

"Where can I find the golden key?" Sea Girl cried, but the wild goose flew off without answering. Sea Girl stamped her foot impatiently.

"What am I to do?" she wondered.

Three parrots sitting in a nearby tree heard her cries. They cocked their heads to one side and stared at her with beady eyes.

"If you want the key..." said one in a rather bored voice.

"...you must search for..." the second continued, yawning.

"...the Third Daughter..." The last parrot spoke so slowly that Sea Girl thought he would fall asleep before he finished.

"...of the Dragon King." Then the three parrots tucked their heads under their wings and fell asleep before Sea Girl had a chance to ask them any more.

"But who is the Dragon King, and where should I look for his daughter?" she wailed.

Sea Girl looked around but no other bird or creature came to help her.

"I shall just have to find the Third Daughter of the Dragon King by myself."

So Sea Girl set off, singing a song about her quest. Many people stopped her along the way to ask about her song, but none could tell her of the Third Daughter of the Dragon King.

After many long and tiring days of walking, Sea Girl met a peacock.

"I have heard your song, Sea Girl," said the peacock. "I know the fortress far away in the Southern Mountains where the Dragon King lives. I will take you there."

Sea Girl thanked the peacock and set off after him, singing her song as she went. She followed him to the crags of the Southern Mountains. There she saw a huge fortress guarded by a fierce and monstrous eagle with huge talons and a pointed beak.

"Here I must leave you," said the peacock. "This is where the Dragon King lives with his daughters. I cannot tell you how to get into the fortress, but I do know that the Third Daughter of the Dragon King loves music. Perhaps if you sing, something will happen."

Sea Girl sat outside the fortress and began to sing. On the first day, she sang all the songs she knew, but the Third Daughter of the Dragon King did not appear. On the second day, she sang all the songs she knew again. Staring up at the fortress, she thought she glimpsed a girl's face at one of the windows. On the third day, Sea Girl started to make up new songs. She sang all day and at last, as the sun began to set, the Third Daughter of the Dragon King appeared beside her. Sea Girl carried on with her songs. Shyly, the other girl joined in, and soon the mountain was filled with the sound of the two friends' voices.

Sea Girl explained her quest to Third Daughter, and Third Daughter agreed to help. She told Sea Girl that the golden key to the secret lake was kept in the left-hand dungeon of the fortress. To reach the dungeon Sea Girl would have to pass the monstrous eagle.

"But how am I to get past him?" asked Sea Girl.

"I have an idea," Third Daughter replied, and she began to explain her plan.

Sea Girl and Third Daughter sang very loudly until the monstrous eagle who guarded the fortress flew over to see what was happening. Third Daughter kept singing, lulling the eagle with her sweet voice, while Sea Girl stole away and crept into the fortress.

The left-hand dungeon was filled with piles of treasure. But Sea Girl turned her back on the gold, jade and jewels and began to look for the key. She spotted it glinting in a dark corner. Clutching the key, she ran from the fortress and made her way back to Third Daughter.

When Sea Girl was safely clear of the fortress Third Daughter stopped singing. The monstrous eagle flew back to the fortress. He did not realize that the golden key was missing because the heaps of gold, jade and jewels that he guarded had not been disturbed.

Sea Girl returned to Horse Ear Mountain with the key. She went to the shining lake and opened it with the golden key. Immediately the water began to flow down from the lake into the river that ran through the village.

From his fortress in the Southern Mountains the Dragon King saw what had happened. He was furious. When he found out how Third Daughter had helped Sea Girl, he banished her from his kingdom forever.

Third Daughter was not very upset by this. Life had been very dull in the Dragon King's fortress and she had been forbidden to sing. So she went to Horse Ear Mountain to live with Sea Girl, and the two girls spent their days singing together.

As for the villagers, when they saw the water flowing into their river, they rushed out of their houses, laughing and crying. They were very grateful to the two girls. One day in every year the ladies of Horse Ear Mountain still sing together by the river to thank Sea Girl and Third Daughter.

29

How We Know

Have you ever wondered how we know so much about the lives of the ancient Chinese, although they lived thousands of years ago?

Evidence from the Ground

Chinese emperors and important officials were often buried in elaborate tombs that contained many everyday objects. Archaeologists can find out a lot about the way these people lived by studying these objects. One tomb contained a life-sized army – 6,000 pottery soldiers and horses, each one with a different face.

Evidence from Books

The Chinese emperors developed a huge administrative system to run their country, and detailed records were made of everything that went on. Many of these records still exist.

▼ An emperor was still living in the Forbidden City up until 1911, so most of it is beautifully preserved.

▲ The pottery army was an extremely useful find for archaeologists.

◀ Records come in all shapes and sizes. This writing is on wood.

Evidence Around Us

Many of the things created by the ancient Chinese survive. The country is still divided into 18 provinces. The Forbidden City and other palaces still stand and tell us much about Chinese architecture. Acupuncture and other forms of medicine invented by the ancient Chinese are still used today.

Glossary

acupuncture
The treatment of illness by sticking small needles into specific places on a person's body.

Analects
The collection of Kung-Fu-tsu's philosophical writings.

Buddhism
The teachings of the Indian prophet Buddha, who died in 483 B.C.

civilization
An organized society that has developed social customs, government, technology and the arts.

civil service
Government departments that administrate the country.

compass
An instrument that shows direction by means of magnetism.

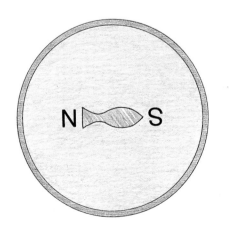

dynasty
A series of rulers all belonging to the same family. The dynasties mentioned in this book are:

Chou 1122 -c.256 B.C.

Qin 221-206 B.C.

Ming A.D.1368-1644

gunpowder
A powder that explodes when lit.

hemp
A plant producing a coarse thread, often used to make rope and sacking.

jade
A hard, green stone used for making jewelry and ornaments.

Kung -Fu-tsu
China's most famous philosopher, who lived during the Chou dynasty. Often known as Confucius in the West.

lacquer
A shiny coating made from oak sap and used to decorate wood.

Lao-tsu
Chinese philosopher who lived during the Chou dynasty.

loess
A fertile, yellow topsoil.

philosopher
A person who seeks wisdom and enlightenment through study and reasoning.

porcelain
A fine-grained type of ceramic used to make china, figurines and other decorative objects.

silk
A fine, soft cloth made from a thread produced by silkworms.

Taoism
The belief that people should live in harmony with nature.

terraces
Flat fields built into the side of a hill like steps to stop the soil from sliding away.

yin and **yang**
Chinese symbols that suggest the opposite sides of nature that together create balance.

Index